brev·i·ty +
clar·i·ty =
au·thor·i·ty

An Entrepreneur's Guide to Growing Revenue
with an Authority Positioning Portfolio™ to
Amplify Your Authority Marketing Strategy

Mike Saunders, MBA

Book Bonus

THE
AUTHORITY POSITIONING
MANIFESTO

A Simple 3-Step PDF Guide to Leverage Your Expertise to Get More Clients and More Profit....Even if You Have Very Little Time & Are Starting from Scratch!

{ALSO} – you will also receive the top 3 video sessions from my Authority & Influence Summit where I interviewed 30 world-class experts who revealed their best strategies to make more impact, dominate your market & establish yourself as the premier expert in your field.

Claim your book bonus at:
www.TheAuthorityPositioningCoach.com

Also By Mike Saunders

1. Authority Marketing for Law Firms
   How to Attract High-Value Cases in Lucrative
   Industries

2. Authority Selling
   Opening More Doors to Closing More Business

3. CA-TA-SA System
   The 1-Page Copyrighted Marketing Strategy

4. Believing Your Why
   The 7-Step "Morning Huddle" System to
   Finally Achieve Your Goals!

5. The PRISM Salvation
   A 3-Step Solution to Social Media Domination for
   Busy Business Owners

Authority Positioning Publishing Strategy by Mike Saunders, MBA
https://www.AuthorityPositioningCoach.com

brev·i·ty +
clar·i·ty =
au·thor·i·ty

brev·i·ty: "concise and exact use of words"

Oxford Dictionary Definition

Why I wrote this book

I WROTE THIS BOOK in the format of "Micro-Publishing."

To distill my specific system and strategy into the most concise length imaginable to clearly communicate my message.

Consider this: In the book *Positioning* by Al Ries and Jack Trout, p.13, they point out that "The Lord's Prayer contains 56 words; the Gettysburg Address, 266; the Ten Commandments, 297; the Declaration of Independence, 300; and a recent U.S. government order setting the price of cabbage, 26,911."

The most impactful messages are brief!

Even though we realize that people want to work with experts, what it takes for us to stand out and be noticed by our target audience has changed dramatically in recent years because we're living in a digital attention-span economy; competition for our prospects' attention is fierce.

When we are looking to make our value proposition clear and compelling, we must remember what New York Times Bestselling author, Donald Miller said in his book, *Building a Story Brand*: "if you confuse you lose." Too many times we find ourselves writing our emails and blog posts or recording our videos and podcasts with so much content that we lose our audience. They just don't have the time to stay attentive.

We must strive to communicate the most compelling key points so that there is no question as to how we can help solve any problem our target audience is facing.

When a strong message must be communicated, keeping it clear and concise is the way to go, but for those who may find themselves struggling to compress their thoughts into such a small amount of content, I recommend placing their thought-leadership content on strategic platforms to enhance trust-building.

We must be seen as the trusted advisor because of where our thought-leadership content is being seen! To illustrate this move to brevity we see in society around us, Amazon haWWs sections called Kindle Short Reads. These are thousands of books that only take 15 minutes to read! Ted Talks are precisely timed to be 18 minutes long, and TV & radio interview segments are typically only 5-12 minutes long.

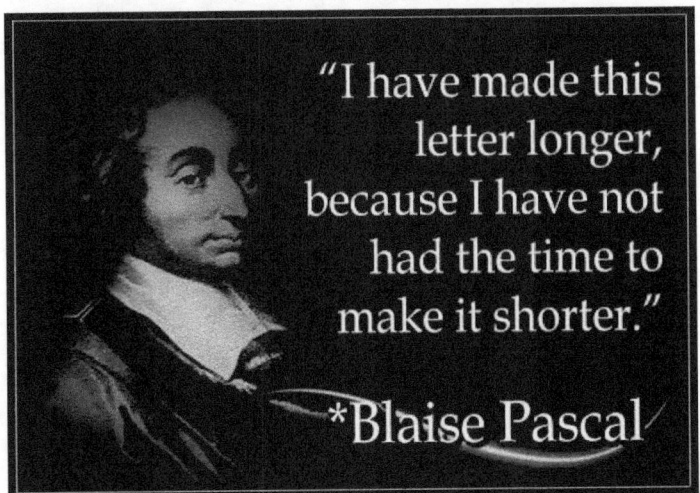

Have you ever heard of, or read, "The Art of War?" It's a book written in the fifth century B.C. by the Chinese general Sun Tzu who is considered one of the most brilliant military strategist and tacticians in history. The strategies in that book have been applied in the world of business, law, finance, politics, and sports. Many executives, CEOs, and successful entrepreneurs consider it one of the most valuable books in their library.

The Art of War is only 64 pages!

It's really about The Art of "Less is More." When you look at very popular books from authors like Charles Dickens, Ernest Hemingway, George Orwell, and titles like:

- *The Science of Getting Rich*
- *Of mice and men*
- *Dr. Jekyll and Mr. Hyde*
- *12 Angry Men*

Just to name a few. Many of these books have been turned into movies. They are all considered classics. They stand the test of time. They also share something else in common:

They are ALL less than one hundred pages.

We need to reset our approach in business communication and marketing to go against the tide and stand out more clearly in our messaging!

This book is strategically designed to be read in one sitting so that you have full and complete understanding of WHY Authority Positioning is critical to grow your business.

{You are welcome!}

Dedication

THIS BOOK IS DEDICATED to all readers who are frustrated with struggling through the latest-and-greatest business book on a topic they need help with...only to reach the end to conclude that the author could have made their main points in less than HALF of the time!

I'm declaring war on the Expert Influencer Industry!

ARE YOU AS SICK-AND-TIRED as I am seeing all of the so-called experts pitching their new course on getting clients... standing in front of "their" luxury sports car...sitting in the driveway of "their" newly purchased mansion?

I mean, it's almost like we can see the rental agreement in the dashboard of the car, and is that multi-million-dollar house really theirs?

Oh...and let's not forget the social media ads we see telling you that they can help scale your business to 7 figures and beyond....and they look 12!

Now, I realize all that is hard to prove, but what I am most frustrated with is the "Expert-Influencer" Industry which has such conflicting approaches to succeed!

Because what you've been told on how you approach, sell, and attempt to obtain high-value clients is complete and utter CONFUSION!

It teaches you to spends countless months, years, and thousands of dollars a month investing in:

1. Copyrighting to dial in your messaging
2. Overhauling your website
3. Daily social media posts on multiple platforms
4. Daily Facebook Live videos
5. Extensive Blogging
6. Weekly Webinars (no matter how many show up - just to practice)
7. Elaborate sales funnels with precise email campaigns
8. Massive investment in Facebook ads to drive leads to your funnel(s)

Take a look over that list again and focus on each one slowly....am I right? Have you seen this being promoted?

To be "10,000 Hours good" in each one, you would need to spend years and invest a massive amount of money learning or hiring the best-of-the-best, to implement it in your business, do you agree?

Conversely, there are others that teach you to have the complete opposite approach which leads you to believe that you can simply set up Facebook ads to drive your perfect prospect to call you on the phone and on that same call, just days after clicking on your ad, you close the deal for a massive fee. (Now don't get me wrong, I have heard both approaches work...and sometimes REALLY well.)

- It's just that I'm sure you, like me, don't have years to lay the groundwork for your expert platform to start delivering results for you.

- And I'm also sure that you are probably not a FB ad and sales guru knowing the precise messaging and ad-spend and high-level sales skills to successfully bring in high-revenue clients days after seeing your ad and close them on the spot.

It does NOT have to be that way!

In this book, I'll be educating you on exactly how to pull your prospects through the Buyers Journey to easily convert them to high-revenue clients while avoiding

"Shiny Object Syndrome" that keeps distracting you with the latest marketing fad!

Are you ready to learn?

About the Author

MIKE SAUNDERS, MBA
AUTHORITY MARKETING STRATEGIST

Mike Saunders is a speaker, bestselling author of four books, and a successful business coach who holds an MBA in Marketing. Mike is also an Adjunct Marketing Professor at several Universities and a member of the Forbes Coaches Council. He has interviewed hundreds of industry experts on his podcast and is always striving to learn from other thought leaders. Mike is most passionate about seeing his family grow up with high spiritual values and providing them opportunities to succeed in life. He is heavily involved in his local church and is focused on teaching others the benefits of giving and serving.

HAS BEEN FEATURED ON
Forbes abc NBC CBS FOX

MIKESAUNDERS360.COM

I empower entrepreneurs to become an instant celebrity by delivering a done-for-you Authority Positioning Portfolio™ of permanent assets on powerful platforms of Publicity, Podcasting, and Publishing.

This creates omnipresence so they are seen as an Expert and Authority in their niche or industry to attract more clients, increase profits and make more impact.

As the #1 Authority Marketing Strategist, My mission is to position you as the #1 authority in your niche or industry to become an instant celebrity & attract more clients, increase your profits, and make more impact.

By building a Christian-based consulting firm, I DO as much as I can to SERVE as much as I can, to MAKE as much as I can so that I can GIVE as much as I can & SUPPORT my family and to provide them life opportunities to succeed.

My Promise to You

WHEN YOU LEARN AND implement this concept of a strategically created "Authority Positioning Portfolio™", you will "pre-frame and post-frame" your unique expertise.

The result will be that you will create and leverage your expertise to effortlessly pull your prospects through the Buyers Journey to easily convert them to new clients & increase your revenues so you can enjoy seeing your brand elevated so far above your competitors that you render them irrelevant & obsolete, making you the obvious choice to your prospects!

Mike runs a 1st-class marketing company, he's helped our business in a great way with marketing, He's a teacher, an encourager, & I can tell you that not only does he have great ideas but those ideas pay off!

James M. Barthel

CEO | MT2 Environmental Engineer

Mike presents a detailed plan for how to position yourself as an expert and have that be a primary driver for people being attracted to what you offer. I am going to recommend to my team we bring Mike on as a consultant.

Richard Shane, PhD

Founder, Sleep Easily, LLC

One Clear Path

THREE SIMPLE STEPS TO create omnipresence so you are seen as an Expert and Authority in your niche or industry to attract more clients, increase profits and make more impact.

Step #1:
Building Your Authority is Your #1 Priority™

RESEARCH CONDUCTED BY AMERICAN social psychologist, Stanley Milgrim *discovered that people trust the people they see as Experts* in their Sphere of Influence. The significance of this study is that he documented and proved the correlation between someone in a position of authority influencing someone else. This is huge implications in business today!

> *You can read about the "shocking" experiment & results in my Forbes piece, just Google: Using the Science of Heuristic Authority Positioning to Leverage Your Expertise to Become the Obvious Choice for Your Prospects*

You must approach building your Authority and Expertise carefully as you do not want to negatively influence your target audience to take advantage of them but remember that people want to work with experts!

Authority Positioning Assets™ position you as a recognized expert in your field making it easy for them to justify the decision to work with you...even if it costs more! Also, you will enjoy seeing the status and prestige of your brand elevated so far above your competitors that you render them irrelevant & obsolete, making you the obvious choice to your prospects!

> *Make sure you have an Authority Positioning content marketing plan because Building Your Authority is Your #1 Priority™*

Step #2:
Dial in the Right Mindset With an Authority Positioning Platform

A "PLATFORM" IS A formal set of principles and goals; so your platform of being an expert thought leader in your industry must be based on a strong foundation for long-term success.

Authority is being an educator and advocate.

- We focus on the success of our prospects and customers
- We empathize with our prospects and customers
- We give value to our prospects and customers
- We solve problems for our prospects and customers
- And we deliver results

And when you think about it that way. You will feel a whole lot more confident. This is what it means to be an expert! When we stop trying to convince people we are the EXPERT, and focus on being a CHAMPION FOR OUR CUSTOMERS, we make it easy for others to call us the EXPERT!

Authorities don't have a job...they have MISSION!

When asked "What do you do"? Translate that question to be "Who do you help"?

- Who is the person that you have the most success helping?
- Who do you enjoy most in helping?
- Who is your perfect prospect?

Next. What do you help them accomplish?

- What is the big outcome that they want to accomplish that you can help them with?

And, How do you help them to accomplish this?

- How are you able to get them from point A to Point B?
- How are you able to fill in the gaps of where they're at to where they want to be or where they need to be?

And then, Why do you help them?

- What is behind your drive?
- What led you to do what you do and help the people that you help?

When you have this mindset, you approach your business from a Higher Purpose!

Bob Burg and John David Mann teach in their wonderful book, "The Go-Giver", a story about the power of giving and serving with added value. I highly recommend this series of books!

For me, I approach Higher Purpose with an added level of focus. By building a Christian-based consulting firm, I DO as much as I can to SERVE as much as I can, to MAKE as much as I can so that I can GIVE as much as I can & SUPPORT my family and to provide them life opportunities to succeed!

Step #3:
You Must Have an Authority Positioning Portfolio™

AN AUTHORITY POSITIONING PORTFOLIO™ is the collection of Authority Positioning Assets™ that show how you guide clients through your plan to empower them succeed.

An Authority Positioning Portfolio™ is a critical tool to have in your business development strategy because:

- it gives you Status and Prestige
- it builds instant trust with your target market
- it pre-frames your Authority & Expertise
- it eliminates the distraction of a full website until the prospect is ready to learn more.

> *The Authority Positioning Portfolio™ is a simple tool that allows you to display quickly and clearly your Authority & Expertise to build instant trust with a prospect.*

I spent about 12 years in the mortgage banking business and I worked a lot with financial advisers and all that time they spoke about their portfolios – their portfolio of stocks and bonds and the types of asset that you can buy. This became ingrained in my mind with my years in the financial services world.

Then in 2008 when I started my digital marketing agency, Marketing Huddle, it really became part of my vocabulary; helping to bring out a way for people to understand something very simply with using a common phrase like "portfolio."

Also, people have a nice connotation with the word "asset" because typically an asset is a good thing; like your house which is something that can appreciate in value. So if we think about our authority, our expertise, our trust, and the transparency and authenticity that we have with our target audience... shouldn't that also be an asset?

With that thought in mind, it's been said that the "Medium is the Message" meaning that WHERE your content is gives as much value as the actual content!

Here's what I mean: Which would you perceive as more reputable?

- A great blog post, or the same content in an article on Forbes or published in a book?
- A YouTube video with extremely helpful information, or the same content on a Podcast on iTunes or Spotify?

See what I mean? We must be seen as the trusted advisor because of where our thought-leadership content is being seen!

These are the categories of content you must have for your Authority Positioning Portfolio™:

1. 3rd Party Authority
2. Auditory Authority
3. Published Authority

In my Celebrity Makr™ Package, I build and deliver these Authority Positioning Assets™ for clients so they have a spectacular Authority Positioning Portfolio™ to grow their business.

The 1st category of 3rd Party Authority includes "Media Mentions."

You cannot just wait around and hope that someone will notice that you're good at whatever you do. Do you realize that when you make decisions, it's based on a lot of psychological triggers?

When the media is talking about you or your business, this gives you instant credibility. Let me say that again. When the media is talking about you or your business, that gives you instant credibility!

Why is that? It's because it's a from a 3rd-party source.

This is a critical piece of the strategy, there are so many messages coming at us individually every day that it's hard for people to tell the difference between what they want to pay attention to and what they should pay attention to.

Do you want to wait and hope that the media might talk about you some day because you've spent years calling yourself an Expert or would you rather have others see you as the Authority & Expert right now because the media is talking about you today?

The next category of 3rd Party Authority includes "Social Proof"

"Social Proof" is one of the many strategies and techniques that marketers rely on to win you over and convince you that their product is worth your hard-earned cash.

It taps into a basic human characteristic – the need to be like others. In our desire to conform, we often succumb and buy whatever marketers have to offer.

"Social proof" is really just a modern name given to something that has existed since humans formed their first communities in the distant past.

What's at work with social proof is more than just the desire to conform or a marketer's attempt to persuade. It's a part of everything we do.

Social proof is ubiquitous and its part of everyone's life. It's a keystone of any marketing strategy and it's a technique you should be incorporating in your plans.

Social proof is simply word-of-mouth. But today we see it most often online in reviews online and on social media. Have you, like me, ever NOT gone to a restaurant because you saw a flurry of bad reviews online? Yep! And take it a step deeper, we didn't even know the people providing those negative reviews...we just trusted them! There is research to back this up, but just observing our own behavior confirms the fact that social proof is HUGE!

The next category of content is Auditory Authority

Remember, you must develop your digital footprint of thought-leadership in a variety of media and platforms. These should include visual (written and video content) and auditory (content your audience can listen to while they do other things)

Have you ever had this happen?

You find a video online about a topic you want to learn about so you start watching it and you decide that you could do other work while you listen to the teaching. But the content creator put their video in a format so once you leave the browser, the video stops! I don't know if you are like me, but that is extremely annoying! I don't need to watch someone's lips move to comprehend what they're saying!

This is the power of podcasting.

Your audience can be listening to your content while they drive, run, exercise, and do other work; and still understand your content! But most importantly they are recognizing you as an educator and advocate and thought leader.

In your Authority Positioning Portfolio™ you must include assets that focus on your Auditory Authority in what I call the "Stealth Sales Interview." This is accomplished either as a guest on another podcaster's show, or when you have your own podcast.

This is where many podcasters miss the mark because they get so enamored with hearing their own voice that they assume that just because they publish a podcast episode their phone will be ringing and there sales funnel will be full...this is not the case! I coach my clients to be very strategic in how they approach each and every podcast interview; in fact, this will shock many podcast experts: I say that it is not all about the numbers, metrics, and downloads... it literally does not matter how many downloads or listens you have!

Why not?

Because when you focus on using each and every episode as a way to leverage your relationships and expert authority positioning, you now have to the KEY to effortlessly pull your prospects through the Buyers Journey to easily convert them to new clients.

> *Would you like to learn how to do this? Just Google: "Optimize The Buyer's Journey Using Strategic Authority Positioning" and read the Forbes article I published where I teach you how to insert powerful Authority Positioning Assets™ into the buyer's journey so that you are the obvious choice!*

The reason I call this approach the "Stealth Sales Interview" is that when you are a guest on a podcast and you focus the conversation on specific areas of interest your target audience struggles with and needs to find a solution for...you are able to educate them while being propped up by the podcast host as the expert!

Let's take it to the Ninja level of Auditory Authority!

Being interviewed is powerful, but to explode your expert status, you must implement what I call the "Audio Expert Maker."

This is where you launch your own podcast. Now stop right there...I can almost hear your moans and groans! I know you have looked into all the confusing steps to set up, launch and produce a podcast....seems like you need an engineering degree to get it done! (Not to mention all the time and effort to maintain it)

I want you to set these fears and frustrations aside just for a moment and imagine if there was a magical podcast mic you rubbed and out popped a "podcast genie" who did all this for you and all you had to do is focus on speaking from your thought-leadership areas of expertise....and having fun doing it!

(I know there is no such thing as a "podcast genie", but my done-for-you podcast production package is pretty close! Reach out and connect with me to discuss)

OK back to the strategy:

With your own podcast your brand is elevated through the stratosphere because YOU are the one interviewing and asking the questions to influencers, thought leaders, and even....get ready for this....your own best prospects!! Say what?

You mean you can interview your prospects on your show? Yep. And they will thank you for it! Then when you have given them this great value, which helps spotlight their business to their prospects, do you think it will be dramatically easier to ask them if you can schedule a brief call to show them an idea you have for them that you think will help their business grow?

I can tell you from experience, the answer is a resounding "YES"!

I have done over 500 episodes on my podcast "Influential Entrepreneurs" and can tell you that this is the perfect business development tool. (If you subscribe on iTunes you will only see 300 episodes shown because for some reason, they cap the number...!)

This is just one Ninja strategy for using your own podcast show as an Audio Expert Maker.

> *If you would like to learn 7 more ways, I did a 37-minute workshop teaching this strategy and you can watch it free and you don't even need to opt in! Just go to www.MikeSaunders360.com click the YouTube icon and you will see "Strategic Podcast Positioning Workshop."*

The next category of content is Published Authority

What sets you apart from your competition? You absolutely must be building a brand in your competitive industry. You must be unique and remarkable, and then you must be able to share that in your messaging online and offline.

Your Authority is your position in the mind of your target audience. When you can articulate your "why", the reason you are in business and passionate about doing what you do, this becomes your brand.

> *Authority Positioning is all about becoming an educator and an advocate for your target audience and putting yourself in their shoes and helping them achieve success.*

When you share value in authoritative and unique ways, your prospects and clients begin to take notice. They call you the Expert or Authority and you never have to. Why is that? Because they're so used to other salespeople or competitors in your industry, who are pushing their products and services on them.

When you come in and begin educating them on their options and choices so that they become an educated buyer of whatever you are selling, they feel the difference. They will respond in a positive way. It has been said in the past, "People don't like to be sold, but they like to buy."

Pause and consider the following scenario. Imagine that the week before an important business meeting or a sales pitch, you send them a book—your book, your bestselling book!

Entrepreneurs are doing exactly that, every day. They're writing, selling and leveraging bestselling books on Amazon, but here is a key strategy to keep in mind: They are not going to make much money from the book in the form of royalties, they are going to make money **because of** the book! Now, you will get paid from Amazon if you decide to publish on their platform, but that is not your focus.

The focus is to use the leverage your book brings to open doors of opportunity for you. Your expertise will be highly regarded by your sphere of influence, target market and industry colleagues. Think about it... what are the 1st 6 letters in the word "Authority"? AUTHOR!

> *Learn more about this powerful strategy in my Forbes piece, just Google: "The Fifth Step In Your Authority Positioning Strategy: Get Published."*

With your polished up marketing messaging and thought-leadership content locked and loaded, you find a way to get published assuming that all of the statistics you have heard will attract new clients to you like crazy....but it has been said that 63% of readers *don't finish reading books*!

When you hand out your book like the best "business card" that it is....just a word of advice: don't contact them a few weeks later and expect that they have read it!

I guide my clients to plan for this reality because it really doesn't matter if your book is read 100%.

Why?

Because you attained to the status of actually having a book. When they see your name on the cover and scan through it a bit....many times, that is all it takes to separate yourself from your competitors who just sent them a color brochure or email campaign!

INTRODUCING:
The BrevityBook™

IT'S NOT ABOUT CREATING a book to sell...it's about creating a book that... SELLS YOU!This style of book is strategically designed to be read in one sitting so that the reader (YOUR PROSPECT) has full and complete understanding of the 1 solution you provide that solves the problem they face!

This book you are holding in your hands is a BrevityBook™ - a special form of "Micro-Publishing" which teaches you my specific system in the most concise length to clearly communicate my message.

> *How would you like to be an Amazon bestselling author with a BrevityBook™ custom designed for your business?*
>
> *Without writing a word!*
> *In 3 hours of your time!*
> *In less than 30 days!*
>
> *Visit: www.AuthorityPositioningCoach.com to schedule your complimentary Discovery Call.*

Once you have built out your Authority Positioning Portfolio™....how do you use it to grow your business?

Imagine getting ready for a sales meeting with a prospect you have been working on landing for months. You realize that this sale would make-or break your quarterly numbers. You finally have the meeting set with their Management Team for next week.

What if you sent each of them an overnight package with a professional cover letter intro expressing how the upcoming meeting will lay out your plan for their success, but in the package, you also include your Authority Positioning Portfolio™:

- Color copies of media mentions you have been featured in
- Testimonials and Reviews from your raving fan clients.
- Flash drive or Video Brochure with 2-3 podcast interviews you have been on as well as interviewing Influencers in their industry that they will recognize.
- A copy of your Amazon bestselling book with a professional color glossy cover featuring your name and picture and the title describes your solution that you provide to customers or companies that have similar problems

When this package arrives a few days before your presentation, and then you arrive for the meeting, are you perceived differently than your competitor that they are also meeting with that week?

This Authority Positioning Portfolio™ can also be delivered electronically for the sales presentations that are not as high-profile. You can set each of those items up on a page on your website with links to each item and send the sales prospect the link in advance of your meeting.

So whether you use it to get the meeting in the first place, or to "Pre-Frame" your presentation before you arrive, or even as a "drop the mic" moment to leave behind after the presentation...you will succeed with this approach!

Take a look at my Authority Positioning Portfolio here:
www.AuthorityPositioningPortfolio.com
(you can click the link at the bottom to set one up for yourself)

Would you like to fast track your Authority Positioning Marketing Campaign?

I will empower you to become an instant celebrity by delivering a done-for-you Authority Positioning Portfolio™ of permanent assets on powerful platforms of Publicity, Podcasting, and Publishing.

This creates omnipresence so you are seen as an Expert and Authority in your niche or industry to attract more clients, increase profits and make more impact.

You'll love knowing that you will be executing what the top 3% of influencers are currently doing to stand out as market leaders. Authority Positioning is the #1 business growth tool for bringing entrepreneurs out of obscurity which results in more clients, more profit, and more impact.

You'll enjoy seeing your brand elevated so far above your competitors that you render them irrelevant & obsolete making you the obvious choice to your prospects!

Visit: www.AuthorityPositioningCoach.com
to schedule your complimentary Discovery Call.

CASE STUDY:

Henry Kaminski, Jr.

*"Mike and his team did all the heavy lifting for me.
All I had to do was focus on what I do best."*

Read Full Case Study at:

https://authoritypositioningcoach.com/portfolio

CASE STUDY:

Dr. Stephen and Janet Lewis

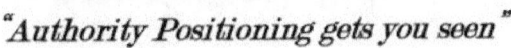

"Authority Positioning gets you seen"

Read Full Case Study at:

https://authoritypositioningcoach.com/portfolio

Implementation Workbook

NOW LET'S PUT WHAT you've learned into action! Take time now to complete this workbook section with carefully thought-out responses.

1. What ONE Problem does your target audience have that you will focus your ONE solution on?

_____

_____

_____

_____

_____

_____

_____

_____

_____

_____

_____

_____

_____

_____

_____

_____

_____

2. How are you the GUIDE and COACH for your client's success?

_____

_____

_____

_____

_____

_____

_____

_____

_____

_____

_____

_____

_____

_____

_____

_____

_____

3. Describe your "Perfect Prospect"? The prospect you have passion/success for helping?

_____

_____

_____

_____

_____

_____

_____

_____

_____

_____

_____

_____

_____

_____

_____

_____

4. Get inside the mind of your prospect and anticipate their real questions, concerns, and fears: List the Top 10 FREQUENTLY asked questions you get about your product or service.

_____

_____

_____

_____

_____

_____

_____

_____

_____

_____

_____

_____

_____

_____

5. List the Top 10 SHOULD asked questions you get about your product or service (these are the deeper questions that if they asked them and understand the answers fully, you are the obvious choice!)

_____

_____

_____

_____

_____

_____

_____

_____

_____

_____

_____

_____

_____

_____

6. What are some common obstacles preventing prospects from achieving this outcome? These can be real or perceived obstacles, the mindset of the prospect, lack of knowledge, or lack of tools.

_____

_____

_____

_____

_____

_____

_____

_____

_____

_____

_____

_____

_____

_____

7. What are the most common fears prospects have about attempting this outcome?

_____

_____

_____

_____

_____

_____

_____

_____

_____

_____

_____

_____

_____

_____

_____

8. What are some myths or misinformation that your prospects may have about achieving the desired outcome?

_____

_____

_____

_____

_____

_____

_____

_____

_____

_____

_____

_____

_____

_____

_____

9. What is your 1 solution you provide your clients to solve their 1 main problem?

_____

_____

_____

_____

_____

_____

_____

_____

_____

_____

_____

_____

_____

_____

_____

_____

10. Are you "interested" or committed"? Detail why NOW is the time for you to finally take action!

_____

_____

_____

_____

_____

_____

_____

_____

_____

_____

_____

_____

_____

_____

_____

www.ingramcontent.com/pod-product-compliance
Lightning Source LLC
Chambersburg PA
CBHW070126230526
45472CB00004B/1433